The ART OF TONY AUTH

TO STIR, INFORM AND INFLAME

TONY AUTH with DAVID LEOPOLD

Camino Books, Inc.
Philadelphia

Manufactured in the United States of America

1 2 3 4   15 14 13 12

Library of Congress Cataloging-in-Publication Data

Auth, Tony.
  The art of Tony Auth : to stir, inform and inflame / Tony Auth with David Leopold.
    p. cm.
  Includes bibliographical references and index.
  ISBN 978-1-933822-71-6 (alk. paper)
  1. United States—Politics and government—1945-1989—Caricatures and cartoons. 2. United States—Politics and government—1989—Caricatures and cartoons. 3. American wit and humor, Pictorial. I. Leopold, David, 1965- II. Title.

E839.5.A87 2012
973.9202'07—dc23   2012024794

Cover and interior design: Jerilyn Bockorick

This book is available at a special discount on bulk purchases for promotional, business, and educational use.

Publisher
Camino Books. Inc
P.O. Box 59026
Philadelphia, PA 19102
www.caminobooks.com

CONTENTS

FOREWORD   Jules Feiffer   iv

INTRODUCTION: A Few Lines on Tony Auth   David Leopold   v

CARTOONS

Vietnam   1

LBJ   12

Washington   16

The Arms Race   26

Nixon   36

Economics   46

Ford   56

Foreign Affairs   62

Carter   72

Guns   82

Energy   94

Reagan   106

Human Rights   116

Bush   142

Faith   152

The Media   162

Clinton   170

Environment   180

Pennsylvania   188

W   198

Us   208

Health Care   218

Obama   228

FOREWORD

Jules Feiffer

The scene is a big city. We are close in on a dark alley. Grimy brick walls lined with sleeping, standing, crouching, disheveled men in old and soiled clothing, two of them huddled for warmth in cardboard cartons, some asleep, some staring into space, all of them resigned. Standing at the entrance of the alley, a bearded man in camouflage hat and fatigues is addressing a down-and-out woman covered in a hood and shawl. He points away from her and says, "This is veterans' housing. The mentally ill are one alley over."

Who but Tony Auth?

The Art of Tony Auth: To Stir, Inform and Inflame—that is the full title of this book. I don't know if it was Tony who came up with the subtitle, or David Leopold or the editor, but it feels right. It has the simplicity and directness that readers will find on just about every page of this perceptive and distinctively American volume.

Tony Auth is a no-nonsense, New Dealish, Frank Capra kind of cartoonist. Five times a week for over 40 years, he clocked in on the editorial page of *The Philadelphia Inquirer* with his unique brand of wit and integrity, served up with an almost martini-like dryness, cooly stirred with iconoclasm and truth. He drew political cartoons that induced the reader to think with a smile, an "Oh wow!" kind of smile, an "If I didn't know this before, I get it now" kind of smile.

Tony believed in—and still believes in—educating as he entertains, and he doesn't like to do one without the other. His fine and exact pen line slices its way to the core of the matter with a deftness and precision that reminds me that he started out as a medical illustrator. His self-assigned mission is to be smart with a heart.

It's in vogue these days to speak of the United States in decline, as in, "Jeez, what a shame you weren't an American when this was a really good country." That is nonsense, of course, but if you look at editorial pages in newspapers today and note the scarcity of editorial cartoons and the lackluster, Leno-like quality of the few that remain, it's easy to see that this art form is very much in decline. From Art Young to Herblock to Mauldin to Conrad to Oliphant, Tony stands as one of our last town criers, doggedly waving his tattered pennant. And even after his old fort has fallen, like Beau Geste, Tony remains at the ramparts.

And for over 35 years I have been privileged to be his friend.

INTRODUCTION

David Leopold

"Our job is not to amuse our readers. Our mission is to stir them, inform and inflame them. Our task is to continually hold up our government and our leaders to clear-eyed analysis, unaffected by professional spin-meisters and agenda-pushers. In these times, when those of us who are members of the "reality-based community" are under relentless attack from both the right and the left, we must encourage, and our work must reflect, independent and non-ideological thinking."

—Tony Auth, in his acceptance
of the Herblock Prize, 2005

From the first, Tony Auth drew pictures to combat difficult times. Bedridden as a child, Tony escaped the confines of his bedroom by listening to radio serials, and was inspired by *The Lone Ranger*, *Superman* and other adventure programs to draw the worlds he only heard. He soon discovered that many of his favorites already appeared in comic books, and it was those pulp publications that became his first art school. Tony would focus on a single radio show and its characters and would learn how to draw them by first copying what he found in comic books, learning anatomy and perspective by osmosis. As he mastered each program, he would move onto the next, copying and creating new storylines for his own amusement.

Tony's vision of himself as a child from *Behind the Lines*, his first book in 1977.

Although Tony knew from an early age that he wanted to draw, he was not sure what he wanted to draw after he graduated from his radio phase. He first attempted political cartooning in the sixth grade, but soon "discovered what was missing was knowledge." He drew the obligatory school scenes for his high school yearbook, and drew gag cartoons on college life for the *Daily Bruin* when he entered UCLA in the fall of 1960, but a *raison d'être* eluded him. He graduated with a degree in biological illustration, and soon found work as a medical illustrator at a nearby teaching hospital.

Tony began, for the first time in his life, to think critically about the current events of his day. The Vietnam War, the civil rights movement and the feminist movement, among other issues, were dominating the headlines and his personal life, particularly the war, as he saw friends drafted and realized his number could come up at any time. He began to study the history of the region and came to the conclusion that the Vietnam War was a terrible mistake. "I started drawing things that meant something to me…and that became political cartooning." He was not alone in being radicalized by the news of the day, and soon friends started a weekly alternative newspaper and asked Tony to be their political cartoonist.

An early cartoon syndicated to alternative weeklies and college newspapers throughout California.

"It is difficult for those who weren't there to imagine just how divided and passionate the country was from the late sixties through the mid-seventies," Tony explained in an interview with the Library of Congress. "We think of America as divided now between red and blue states. During Vietnam the divide was generational, with families torn apart, some parents not speaking to their children, and some young people burning their draft cards or fleeing to Canada. And the civil rights movement, desegregation orders, Martin Luther King's assassination, the rise of the Black Panthers, and a new women's movement all provided incendiary ink for cartoonists. I have long believed that political cartoonists are born of social upheaval, and that generations of unrest gave us, among others, Jeff MacNelly, Garry Trudeau, Mike Peters and Doug Marlette."

Tony was inspired by Herb Block, whose cartoons for the *Washington Post* were syndicated far and wide, and closer to home, Paul Conrad, who had replaced, in Tony's words, "the bland and predictable" Bruce Russell at the *Los Angeles Times*. "Paul Conrad came to the *Times* from the *Denver Post*, and, in a move that would change the history of American political cartooning, the *Denver Post* hired a young Australian named Pat Oliphant as their staff cartoonist," as Tony remembers. "What a turn-on their work was for a young, aspiring cartoonist. I was now reading voraciously, and therefore seeing the work of Herblock, Jules Feiffer, David Levine and others who were creating inspired, funny, beautiful, angry and, above all, honest images. As my commitment to political cartooning became a passion, I began to feel I was part of a raucous and iconoclastic fraternity of commentators, most of whom I would not meet for several years."

After a year of work on a weekly cartoon, syndicated by Sawyer Press to alternative weeklies and school newspapers all through California, in 1966, at the age of 24, Tony decided to call Paul Conrad at the *Los Angeles Times* and ask for an evaluation of his work. "C'mon on down, kid!" Conrad responded. "I showed up with some 50 drawings," Tony recalled in his eulogy at Conrad's funeral in 2010.

"He started going through them, and after looking at nine or ten, I thought I saw a kind of weight lift from his shoulders. 'They're not bad, kid!' Then, with the same unvarnished honesty he daily applied to his cartoons (how could it be otherwise?), he proceeded to give me the best advice I've ever gotten.

'You do one cartoon a week?'

'Yes, sir.'

'And it sits on your drawing board for three or four days, right?'

'Right.'

'Kid, you're loving these drawings to death. A political cartoon has to look like you read the paper, got mad, sat down and in one furious and energetic bout of drawing got your anger out of your system and had a good laugh at the same time. If a reader's first reaction is, 'Boy, this drawing was a lot of work,' they'll be too tired to look any further. Another thing: Anybody can do one cartoon a week. You've got to find out if you have five a week in you.'"

"It's my draft notice…"

"SEEMS LIKE WE GOT A CIVIC DUTY TO RIOT !"

Tony took the advice about simplicity and frequency and returned to the *Daily Bruin*, where for the next six years he published three cartoons a week. He continued to look for a bigger newspaper to reach a wider audience. An editor in Riverside, California couldn't get approval to hire Tony because syndicated cartoons were so inexpensive, but he did send samples of Tony's work to the Chicago Tribune–New York News Syndicate, which recognized the quality and started to let Tony know of possible openings on newspapers around the country. The syndicate gave him several contacts at regional papers. When he was told of an opening at a paper in Honolulu, Tony quickly sent off his best pieces. He received a one-sentence response. "When and if you grow up, there might be a place for you in American journalism." He had sent his anti-war cartoons and other left-wing subjects to a paper whose primary audience worked at the military base there.

In 1971, Tony was alerted by the syndicate to an opening at the *Philadelphia Inquirer*, which had recently been purchased by publisher and editor John S. Knight. The paper, the town's definite "second read," was looking for an unknown cartoonist who could be a distinct voice as the paper remade itself into just the type of major urban daily paper that Tony wanted to work on. He dutifully sent off a résumé and cartoon samples. His rejection letter told him he was talented but "too liberal" (which his syndicate contact told him later meant that they feared he was a "bomb thrower"). Tony then contacted the editorial page editor, Creed Black, and asked to be sent the paper so that he could see the kind of editorial page the paper was producing. After a week or so, Tony called Black and said while the paper's editorials were more conservative, he felt that they were not that far apart since the *Inquirer* was printing Herblock and Bill Mauldin." Creed Black, a moderate Republican who had served in the first Nixon administration, understood that his world was changing, and while he did not agree with Tony's viewpoint, he thought it might be important to include.

Black decided to explore the matter further, and Tony was flown to Philadelphia for a week-long job interview "where my task was to attend the editorial board meetings, take positions, argue my point of view, win some arguments and lose others. In short, for a week, I did everything a political cartoonist does at a newspaper…except draw cartoons." After the week was finished, they sent him home with no offer. Tony returned to Los Angeles, wondering "if this dream was going to materialize or not." Three days later, though, Black called and told Tony, "when you got on that plane, we heaved a sigh of relief, but…we discovered we missed you. Your point of view is valid. It ought to be represented in our editorial discussions. Nobody will tell you what to draw, but I will have veto power."

Tony was hired on the condition that he provide a choice of cartoons each day for Black to choose from. "Creed would never tell me what to draw, he said, but wanted a choice of drawings to pick from," Tony reminisced. "That led to some game-playing by the two of us. If I had what I thought was a really good drawing, and he picked one of the other two sketches I submitted that day, I would show up the next day with the remaining two. If he picked the 'wrong' one again, I would only submit the one he'd turned down twice on the third day, and we'd fight about it. I lost a fair number of those fights, but also won my share." Six weeks after Tony arrived at the *Inquirer*, he was offered a national syndication contract, extending his reach and impact across the country.

FRANK RIZZO - THE LITTLE KING

As Tony continued to prove himself with cartoons on both national and local subjects, he came to an understanding with Creed Black, and by the time Tony won the paper's second Pulitzer Prize in 1976, he was submitting one piece a day, just like any regular contributor. From the ten cartoons he submitted with his entry, the Pulitzer committee cited his July 22, 1975 cartoon, "O beautiful for spacious skies, for amber waves of grain," showing Soviet leader Leonid Brezhnev in a wheat field. While the half-life of that cartoon—a wry comment on the large sale of American wheat to Russia to keep its people fed—is long past, the committee was recognizing Tony's everyday brilliance in getting to the heart of his subject with an engaging cartoon that did not demand attention through bravura line work, but commanded attention by its moral authority, fine line and sense of humor.

"Political cartooning in our country is divided into basically two groups," says Tony. "Those like Herblock, who think that political cartooning is serious work, don't shy away from doing a

'O beautiful for spacious skies
For amber waves of grain . . . '

cartoon that's sad or poignant. The other group thinks that the primary role of cartooning is to provide laughter. It's not like they're two distinct groups; it's just that people like Herblock are not afraid of making their point in the absence of humor, if that's what it took." Tony is firmly in the Herblock camp. Humor is but one weapon in his arsenal.

Drawings such as "Memorial Day" (page 6) reveal a citizen artist. A vet touches the names on Maya Lin's Vietnam Memorial and is in contact with a member of the country's first volunteer army from the American Revolution. When the drawing was published in 1988, it may have referred to a Vietnam vet, but today that vet could have served in Iraq or Afghanistan. Fifty years from now it will summon different wars, but the idea will remain the same: both men fought for their country. Tony's cartoons reflect a respect for our soldiers, and even in his earliest Vietnam cartoons, he never criticized them, but rather the leaders. Tony maintains a high bar for all leaders. He believes they should know better, which adds to his indignation, whether it be about the economy or the arms race.

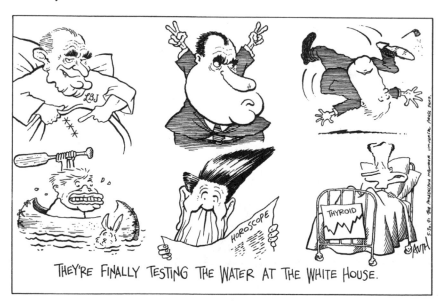

THEY'RE FINALLY TESTING THE WATER AT THE WHITE HOUSE.

There have been nine presidents in the White House during Tony's career, beginning with
Lyndon Johnson. Each new administration provides new characters for his pen and new issues
to address in his cartoons. His work begins during the elections, and that involves not only the
candidates, but the press that covers them, and voters themselves and their level of engagement.
Like any citizen, Tony wants the President to succeed in his role as leader of the country. He
holds the Oval Office to high standards, whether the occupant be Democrat or Republican.
Depending on their action or inaction, he criticizes those he supports, and supports those he
criticizes as warranted.

"I don't try and be balanced," Tony says and laughs, "I try to tell the truth as I see it. I don't
try to be evenhanded in the sense that I offset myself by contradicting something that I said
yesterday. This medium is about making one point at a time, and I want to be part of the argument. When I get mail from readers asking me to be evenhanded, I ask them who their favorite

THE LOSER

columnist is and do they expect them to be evenhanded. No, the goal is to try and tell the truth. I would be the last person to say I succeed all the time. When you do try and do that, you are going to be critical of people and issues you support from time to time. You can support Israel, for instance, and still be very critical of what its government does. Just like in America. The bane of our existence is the assumption that if you are critical of a certain administration that you are somehow un-American."

Tony sees himself as a journalist, a commentator who works graphically. His moral code is not dogmatic but rooted in fairness, particularly for the less fortunate and oppressed. Of all the issues that Tony has addressed over the years, human rights and equality for all people, regardless of race, gender or sexuality, have been at the heart of his work. The civil rights struggle of his youth was one of the issues that spurred him into editorial cartooning. This was quickly succeeded by the women's movement, followed by the fight for gay rights, both of which Tony sees as a natural extension of the civil rights movement.

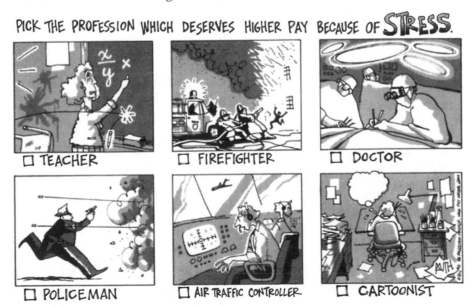

While the civil rights and women's rights movements were already under way when Tony joined the fray, he was an early public supporter of gay rights. His cartoons in the 1970s, when few other cartoonists or columnists were addressing the issue, led some to believe that Tony was gay because, they assumed, who else would champion that fight? Although he is not gay, black, Hispanic or a woman, Tony has used the "power of his pulpit" to advocate for their causes. We can trace how far we have come, and how far we have to go, by looking at his cartoons.

That look at the cartoons reveals no distinct style. Although all of them are unmistakably by Tony, he has never let a signature style interfere with his message. "I always start with a clean sheet of paper, and the goal is to marry the way a drawing is done to the idea that you are trying to express. You don't want to do a whimsical drawing of a mass murderer. That understanding leads to variation of style." Tony took Paul Conrad's advice seriously, and he prizes simplicity in his cartoons, often eliminating extraneous details or even backgrounds to allow his cartoons to have the most impact. Occasionally, Tony finds that a finely detailed drawing is the answer to that day's graphic question, but at heart, he is more interested in spontaneity than preciseness.

Recognizing that his rough sketches had more life than some of his finished drawings, Tony started to use a light box to trace the rough, allowing him to keep the essence of the sketch in the finished work. "I've been on a quest to capture the spontaneity of my loose sketches," Tony told one interviewer. "In any sort of drawing where your goal is communicating, much of the goal is determining what to leave out."

One thing Tony has never left out of his drawings is hope. One of the drawbacks to a long career is that the same issues continue to crop up over and over again, yet Tony has never become cynical: "Cynical cartoonists are boring. To do this work, you have to be optimistic." Does his work help to bring about change, progress or reform? "Yes, but only in the sense that any of us contributes one particle a day to the torrent of news, opinion, argument, spin, exaggeration and lies that people are exposed to constantly," explains Tony. "All that any of us who comment on 'current events' want to do is to be part of the robust and ongoing conversation of American democracy. We say what we have to say, as best we can, and we expect disagreement, controversy and tumult. As the great Bill Mauldin once remarked, 'When you do this for a living, you get two things—awards and hate mail.'"

In 2005, Tony accompanied writer John Timpane of the *Philadelphia Inquirer* on a series that took the two out of the office and into a number of Philadelphia institutions to write and draw what went on before the public arrived. "We spent a week with the orchestra, going to every rehearsal, and then a concert at the Kimmel," Tony recalled in his farewell to the *Inquirer* after 41 years at the end of March 2012. "John wrote a wonderful piece, and I did 50 or so drawings. There was room for eight or nine drawings in the paper, but we posted most of them on the website. We did the same thing for, among others, the Phillies, the Flower Show and the Philadelphia Zoo. The drawings were very different from political cartoons, and were rewarding in an entirely different way. I have illustrated a number of children books and even comic strips, but I began to think then about making room in my role as a journalist for different forms of expression."

The idea germinated when Tony discovered an iPad app, "Brushes," after seeing a David Hockney *New Yorker* cover using the same app, which also records every stroke an artist makes, and allows the finished drawing to be played back as a movie. Tony added a voiceover and began to experiment in this new digital realm, first on the *Inquirer*'s website, and now these experi-

ments have fully flowered at Philadelphia's public broadcasting affiliate, WHYY's NewsWorks website, where Tony is the digital artist-in-residence. This dynamic experience allows him to interact with his audience in a way a static image on the printed page cannot, making it a natural for the online world, and him a pioneer in what may be the future for editorial cartooning. Tony continues to supply three drawings a week for syndication, and does illustrations for the website as well, so despite leaving a coveted, five-cartoon-a-week perch at the *Inquirer*, his audience can actually see more of his work than ever.

"Who are the cartoonists being born of the current battles in American politics?" asks Tony. "We don't yet know, of course, but they will emerge. A more intriguing question, and one which cannot as yet be answered, is where their work will appear, and whether they will be able to make a living at it. This has always been a tiny profession. It requires, after all, a fairly rare confluence of talent, interests and temperament. Forty-one years ago, when the *Philadelphia Inquirer* hired me, there were 200 of us doing daily political cartoons. Now, with newspapers losing circulation and looking for ways to save money, our number is less than 80. We know a couple of things for sure. There will always be artists doing impolite, raucous, iconoclastic and irreverent political drawings. And nothing could be more American."

Many Tony Auth cartoons tell us more than columns of newsprint in a way that we remember them long after other viewpoints have faded. His seemingly unflappable optimism and unwillingness to bow to power give us all a voice in the issues of the day. Tony might not show us or our leaders at our best, but there is always his hope that we will be the better for it.

"I've gotta stop smoking grass.
It makes me paranoid."

News item: One hundred GI deaths per week in Vietnam is considered an acceptable level by the Administration.

Pick the draft dodger.
©1974, PHILADELPHIA INQUIRER C.T.N.Y.N.S.
AUTH
HE FEIGNED ILLNESS.
HE TOOK DRUGS THAT RAISED HIS BLOOD PRESSURE.
HE STAYED IN SCHOOL 12 YRS.
HE GOT MARRIED.
HE PRETENDED TO BE GAY.
HE OBJECTED TO THE WAR ON MORAL GROUNDS AND WENT TO CANADA.

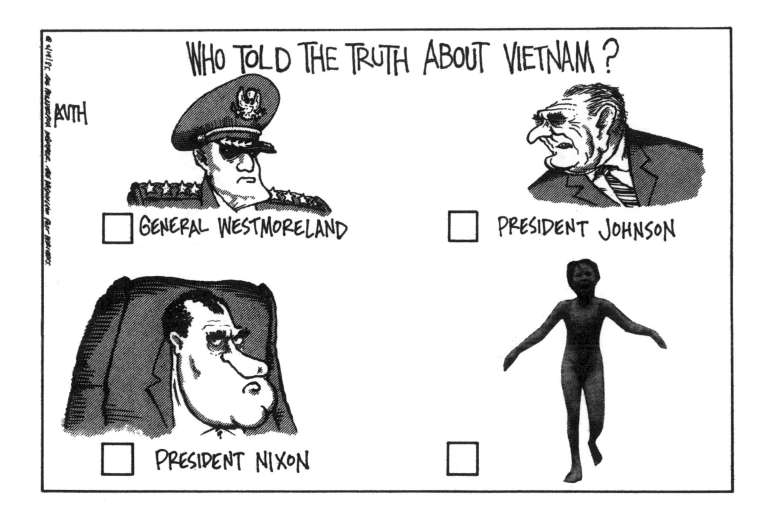

Domino Theory

LBJ

"And for you, young man..."

10·29·09 THE PHILADELPHIA INQUIRER. UNIVERSAL UCLICK.

VIETNAM, BY LYNDON B. JOHNSON

"VICE PRESIDENT BIDEN REDECORATED YOUR OFFICE."

WASHINGTON

6·14·90 THE PHILADELPHIA INQUIRER. UNIVERSAL PRESS SYNDICATE.

2·26·08 THE PHILADELPHIA INQUIRER. UNIVERSAL PRESS SYNDICATE

"THIS IS VETERANS' HOUSING. THE MENTALLY ILL ARE ONE ALLEY OVER."

THE INCUMBENT

IN

OUT

THE ARMS RACE

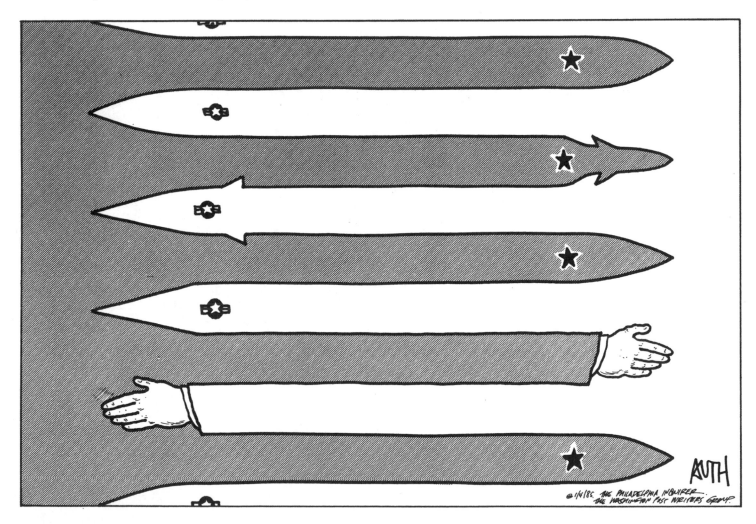

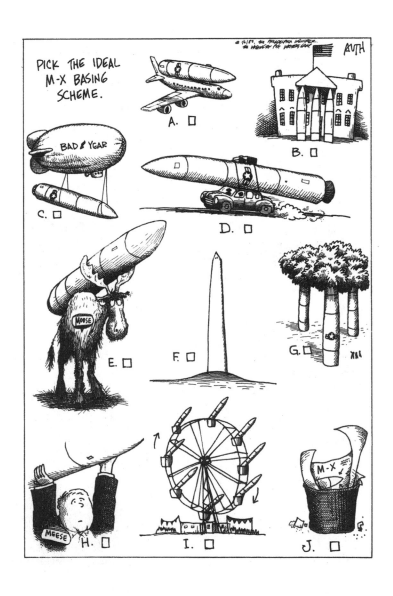

MoRe 'UNTHINKABLES'

A SOVIET MISSILE ATTACK ON THE U.S.

A WARSAW PACT INVASION OF WESTERN EUROPE.

A SOVIET INVASION OF POLAND.

SERIOUS CUTS IN THE U.S. DEFENSE BUDGET.

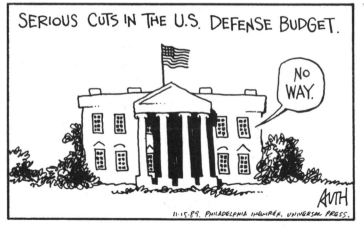

NO WAY.

11-15-89. PHILADELPHIA INQUIRER. UNIVERSAL PRESS.

AUTH

THE MEEK INHERITING THE EARTH

NIXON

"At last...mine...ALL mine!"

'You're doing very well in foreign affairs, Richard,
but your homework is abominable!'

State of the Union

'It works!'

'The wages of sin are fantastic!'

ECONOMICS

'He's a lot less concerned about unemployment
since he got the job <u>he</u> wanted.'

FORD

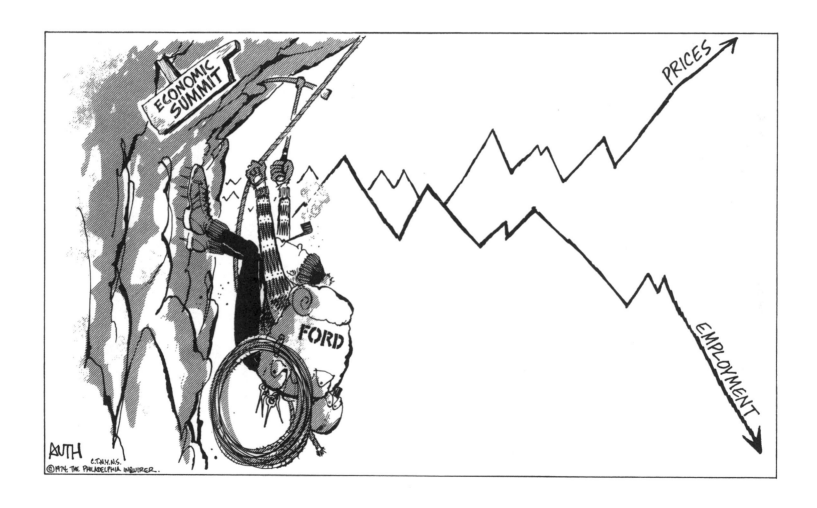

'At least he's a realist.'

'Now to shut the book on Watergate . . .'

'Nevermore!'

FOREIGN AFFAIRS

AUTH

PAX AMERICANA

9/22/02 THE PHILADELPHIA INQUIRER. UNIVERSAL PRESS SYNDICATE.

'I'll stop when you do.'

SHE ASKED FOR IT.
SHE WORE A TIGHT SWEATER.

HE ASKED FOR IT.
HE BOUGHT A BMW.

THEY ASKED FOR IT. THEY MOVED
INTO A WHITE NEIGHBORHOOD.

HE ASKED FOR
IT. HE PUT IN
A GOVERNMENT
I DON'T LIKE.

4.3.02 THE PHILADELPHIA INQUIRER. UNIVERSAL PRESS SYNDICATE.

9/2/09 THE PHILADELPHIA INQUIRER. UNIVERSAL UCLICK.

CARTER

Washington

Lincoln

Teddy Roosevelt

Carter

'I WON'T DEBATE JOHN ANDERSON — HE'S A MERE MEDIA CREATION!'

GUNS

Head Start Program

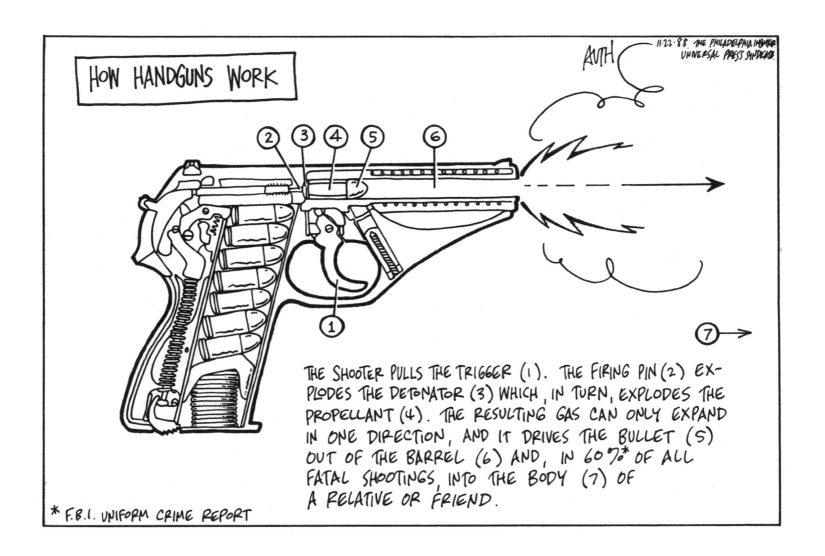

HOW HANDGUNS WORK

THE SHOOTER PULLS THE TRIGGER (1). THE FIRING PIN (2) EX-
PLODES THE DETONATOR (3) WHICH, IN TURN, EXPLODES THE
PROPELLANT (4). THE RESULTING GAS CAN ONLY EXPAND
IN ONE DIRECTION, AND IT DRIVES THE BULLET (5)
OUT OF THE BARREL (6) AND, IN 60%* OF ALL
FATAL SHOOTINGS, INTO THE BODY (7) OF
A RELATIVE OR FRIEND.

* F.B.I. UNIFORM CRIME REPORT

3-7-01 THE PHILADELPHIA INQUIRER. UNIVERSAL PRESS SYNDICATE.

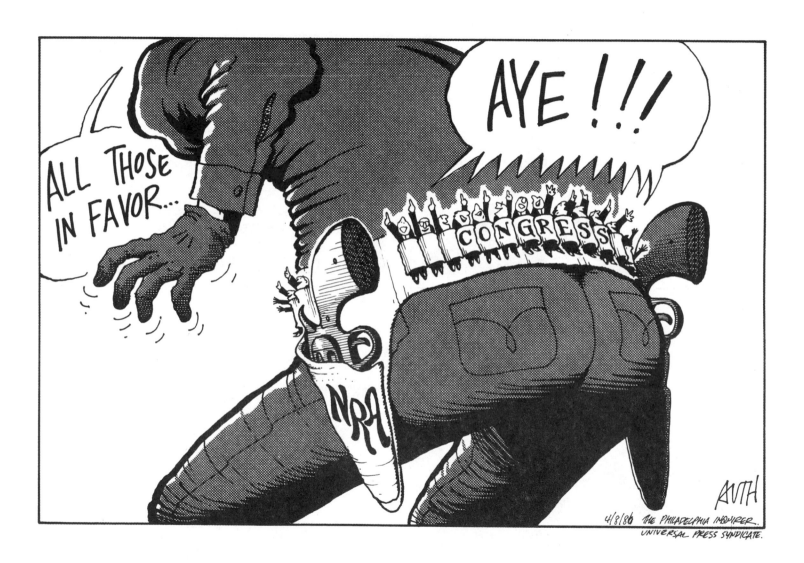

5.12.06 THE PHILADELPHIA INQUIRER.

3·4·10 THE PHILADELPHIA INQUIRER. UNIVERSAL UCLICK.

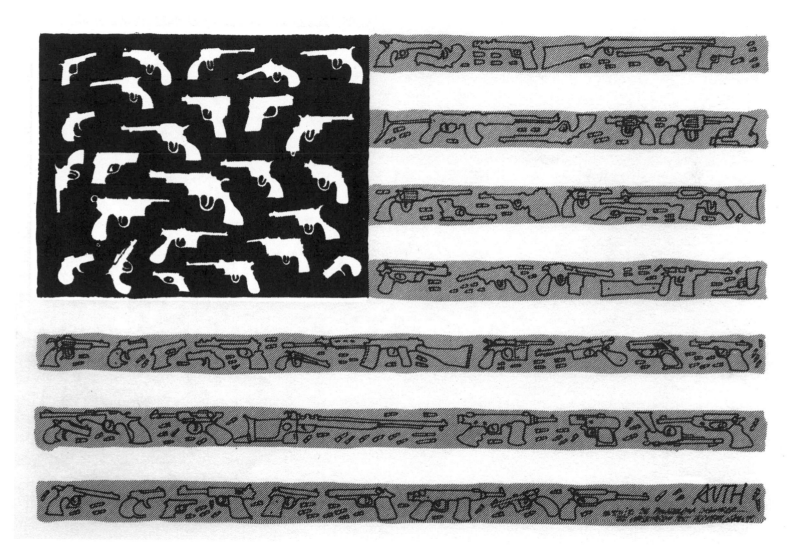

ENERGY

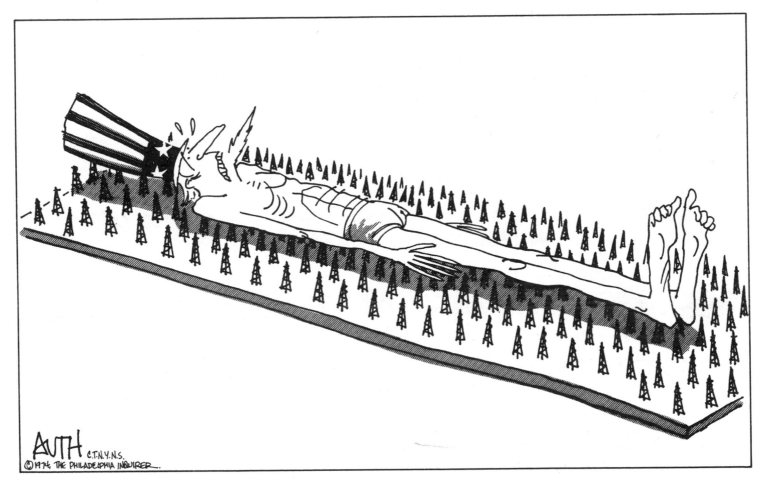

'Nuclear waste problem? I don't know about you, but I don't want my kids growing up in a world where there aren't any problems left to solve!'

'I'm afraid the price has gone up again.'

5·2·10 THE PHILADELPHIA INQUIRER. UNIVERSAL UCLICK.

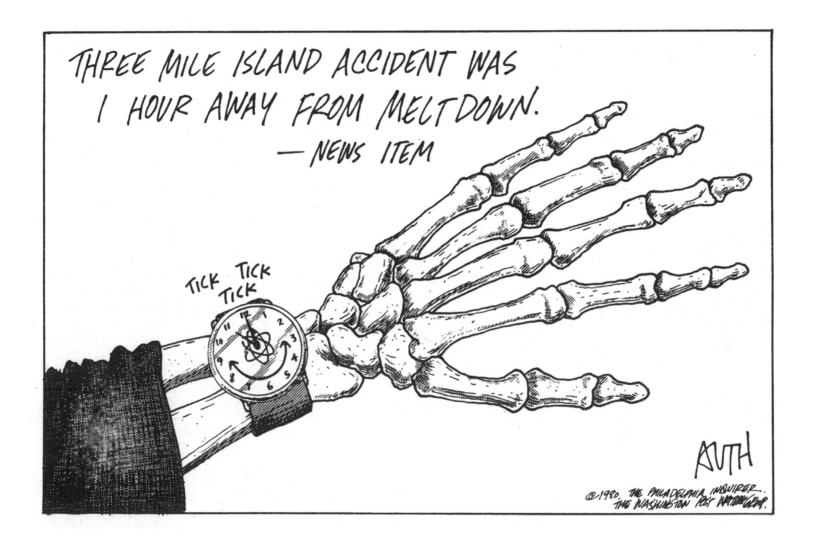

PICK THE SINGLE MOST SERIOUS THREAT TO THE NUCLEAR INDUSTRY:

☐ A.　　　　☐ B.

12·13·11 THE PHILADELPHIA INQUIRER. UNIVERSAL UCLICK.

REAGAN

RONALD AND GLADYS
ARE SENIOR CITIZENS...

THEY BOTH HAVE
SUBSIDIZED MEALS...

AND HOUSING...

AND PUBLIC TRANSPORTATION.

YOU CAN JUDGE
A SOCIETY BY
THE WAY IT
TREATS ITS
AGED !

AUTH
© 12/6/81. THE PHILADELPHIA INQUIRER
THE WASHINGTON POST WRITERS GROUP.

2·15·89. THE PHILADELPHIA INQUIRER. UNIVERSAL PRESS SYNDICATE.

HUMAN RIGHTS

AUTH

© 1/31/89 THE PHILADELPHIA INQUIRER
THE WASHINGTON POST WRITERS GROUP

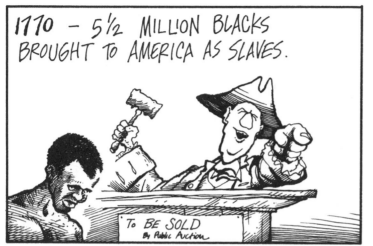

5·29·09 THE PHILADELPHIA INQUIRER. UNIVERSAL PRESS SYNDICATE.

7.30.10 THE PHILADELPHIA INQUIRER. UNIVERSAL UCLICK.

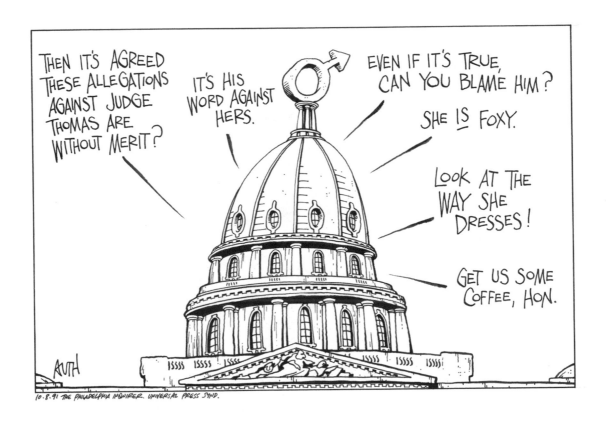

'I'm sorry, but I don't rent to Bible-toting fanatics . . . I
don't want my kids influenced by them.'

THE HISTORY OF THE "DON'T ASK-DON'T TELL" POLICY

5.28.10 THE PHILADELPHIA INQUIRER. UNIVERSAL UCLICK.

THERE ARE NO HOMOPHOBES IN FOXHOLES.

© 1976, THE PHILADELPHIA INQUIRER.
THE WASHINGTON POST WRITERS GROUP.

AUTH

EQUAL JUSTICE UNDER LAW

ANTI-GAY RULING

'...except for them pre-verts.'

BUSH

2·27·92 THE PHILADELPHIA INQUIRER. UNIVERSAL PRESS SYND.

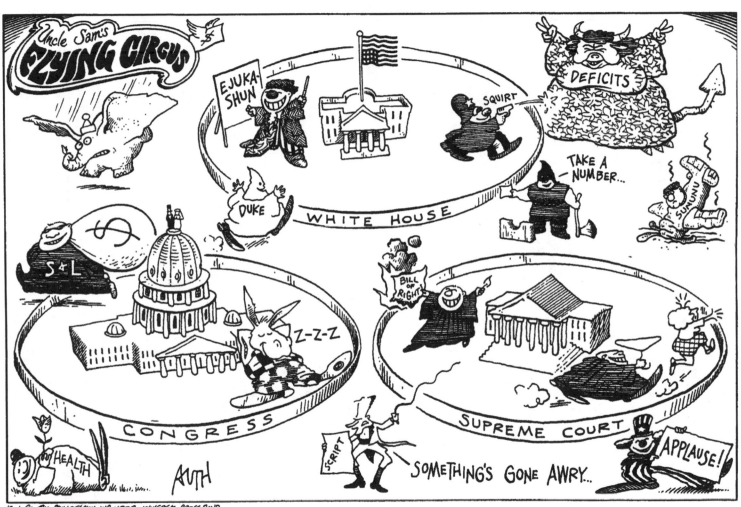

FAITH

"How can you suggest that we evolved from the lowly fish? We're much too special!"

2·29·04 THE PHILADELPHIA INQUIRER. UNIVERSAL PRESS SYNDICATE.

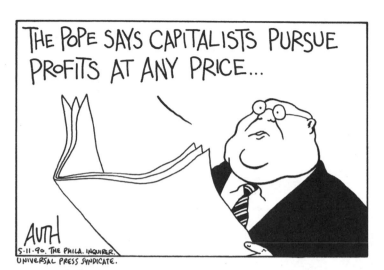

3.19.09 THE PHILADELPHIA INQUIRER. UNIVERSAL PRESS SYNDICATE.

THE MEDIA

'Lights! Camera! . . . Election!'

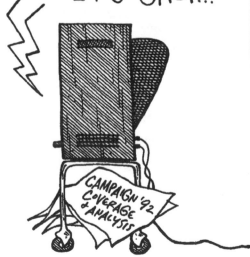

4.20.08 THE PHILADELPHIA INQUIRER. UNIVERSAL PRESS SYNDICATE.

TRIVIAL PURSUIT

3.4.09 THE PHILADELPHIA INQUIRER. UNIVERSAL PRESS SYNDICATE.

6·14·09 THE PHILADELPHIA INQUIRER. UNIVERSAL PRESS SYNDICATE.

CLINTON

WHAT GOES THROUGH A PRESIDENT'S MIND WHEN THE <u>WRONG</u> <u>SPEECH</u> COMES UP ON THE TELEPROMPTER?

9-26-93 THE PHILADELPHIA INQUIRER. UNIVERSAL PRESS SYNDICATE.

11.5.98 THE PHILADELPHIA INQUIRER. UNIVERSAL PRESS SYNDICATE.

8·16·00 THE PHILADELPHIA INQUIRER. UNIVERSAL PRESS SYNDICATE.

ENVIRONMENT

'Vietnam, Watergate, inflation, recession . . . what next?'

'How can the youth of our country be proud of our mining
industry if they can't see it from our national parks?'
                    — Dan Miller, assistant secretary of the interior

4.22.11 THE PHILADELPHIA INQUIRER. UNIVERSAL UCLICK.

PENNSYLVANIA

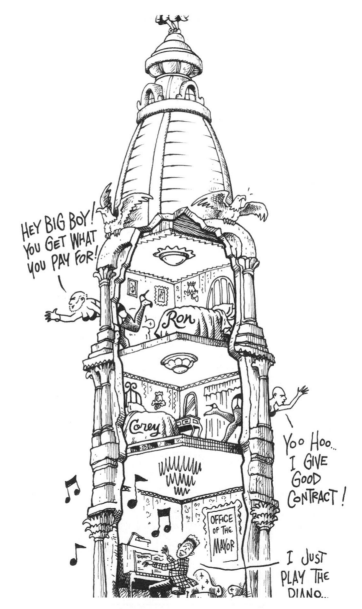

'YOU'RE DAMN RIGHT I TOOK BRIBES AND KICKBACKS AND USED MY OFFICE FOR PERSONAL PROFIT...THIS IS PENNSYLVANIA! AND BY THE WAY, I WANT MY PENSION.'

Matisse, Henri, *The Dance II*. 1932. The Barnes Foundation.

10.8.09 THE PHILADELPHIA INQUIRER.

11·9·11 THE PHILADELPHIA INQUIRER. UNIVERSAL UCLICK.

VOTING RECORD

CHENEY

AUTH

7-28-00 THE PHILADELPHIA INQUIRER. UNIVERSAL PRESS SYNDICATE.

1·31·01 THE PHILADELPHIA INQUIRER. UNIVERSAL PRESS SYNDICATE.

1.7.10 THE PHILADELPHIA INQUIRER. UNIVERSAL UCLICK.

10/20/04 THE PHILADELPHIA INQUIRER. UNIVERSAL PRESS SYNDICATE

1.14.09 THE PHILADELPHIA INQUIRER. UNIVERSAL PRESS SYNDICATE.

US

10.17.00 THE PHILADELPHIA INQUIRER. UNIVERSAL PRESS SYNDICATE.

'I just love Thanksgiving!'

THERE IS TRULY A WIZARD IN OUR MIDST.

10.2.09 THE PHILADELPHIA INQUIRER. UNIVERSAL UCLICK.

HEALTH CARE

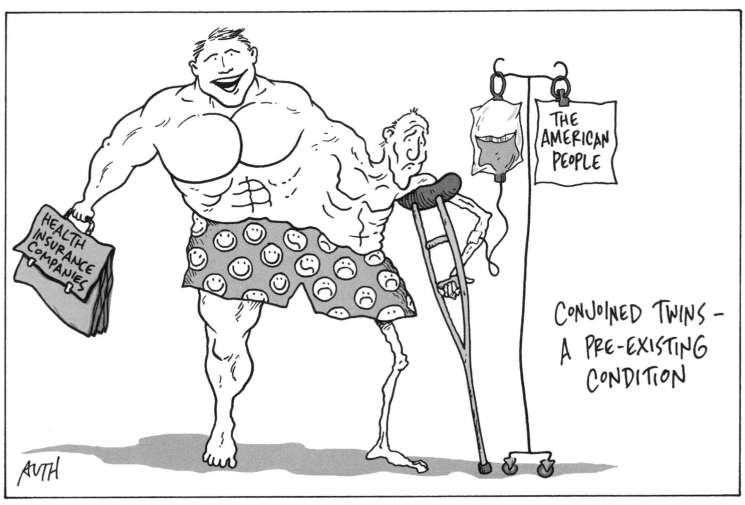

6·21·09 THE PHILADELPHIA INQUIRER. UNIVERSAL PRESS SYNDICATE.

CONGRESS SAVES HEALTH CARE REFORM

6.5.09 THE PHILADELPHIA INQUIRER. UNIVERSAL PRESS SYNDICATE.

9/13/09 THE PHILADELPHIA INQUIRER. UNIVERSAL UCLICK.

"JUST HAVE A SEAT. YOU'LL HAVE TO WAIT."

9.22.10 THE PHILADELPHIA INQUIRER. UNIVERSAL UCLICK.

1·18·09 THE PHILADELPHIA INQUIRER. UNIVERSAL PRESS SYNDICATE.

10·23·11 THE PHILA. INQUIRER. UNIVERSAL UCLICK.

HE WASN'T, YOU KNOW, BORN IN AMERICA.

HE'S NOT, YOU KNOW, A CHRISTIAN.

HE'S, YOU KNOW, A MUSLIM OR A KENYAN.

HE'S, WELL, YOU KNOW...

4.26.11 THE PHILADELPHIA INQUIRER. UNIVERSAL UCLICK.

9·17·09 THE PHILADELPHIA INQUIRER. UNIVERSAL UCLICK.

"RACISM HAS NOTHING TO DO WITH THIS."

12·8·11 THE PHILADELPHIA INQUIRER. UNIVERSAL UCLICK.